Humanity-At-Its- Best
A Truth Seeker's Guide to Living a Principled Life

Glenn Hoffarth

Ice Age Trail Publishing House—Madison, WI
ISBN: 979-8-2183291-2-9
Library of Congress Control Number: 2023923520
Title: *Humanity-At-Its- Best: A Truth Seeker's Guide to Living a Principled Life*
Author: Glenn Hoffarth
Digital distribution | 2023
Paperback | 2023

Dedication

This book would not be possible without the patience and support of my wife Julieann, the inspiration from my empathetic children Jarod and Lauren, and the countless wise people, from cultures around the globe, who have lived throughout history and today, that have inspired their community members to live a more virtuous and harmonious life.

Introduction

Throughout history there have been individuals who have asked their contemporaries to reflect on the moral climate of their society. More than twenty-five centuries ago, Confucius called his fellow citizens to improve their conduct so that they might be considered examples of "Manhood -at-it's-Best." At approximately the same time, in the Mediterranean, Socrates was beseeching Athenians to lead lives based on self-examination, so that they might discover what was good and just. During other epochs, other spiritual leaders such as Lao Tzu, the Buddha, Jesus, Mohammed, and Gandhi, did much the same. In the present age, there are religious leaders, philosophers, journalists, educators, and government officials who act as "voices in the wilderness"; constantly calling on humanity to pause and reflect. Humanity is, and will continue to be, indebted for their efforts. But it is not just for special men and women to rally humanity to improve itself. It is also for the common person, the ordinary world citizen, to assume the responsibility of making the world a better place to live. I am such a person, with no special qualifications other than my love for humanity. The words which follow represent the limited knowledge I have acquired in my journey through life. My intent is to look at the past experiences of great men and women and to use their insights as a source of wisdom for dealing with current problems. It is by no means the only way. Human beings will always find new ways to overcome obstacles. But past experience has always been a useful tool in problem solving. It is my hope that the wisdom of the past will provide guidance for people living in the present to become "Humanity-at-its-Best."

Although the quest to achieve Humanity-at-its-Best can be undertaken by anyone it should be understood that the ability to undertake the endeavor and to succeed will be influenced by social factors. We know that recommendations to eat healthy food, made by doctors and nutritionists, are often difficult to meet for those who are poor or who live in a "food desert." This reality may make it difficult for those who are poor or suffer some other social illness to be able to follow all of the principles of Humanity-at-its-Best. This difficulty must be acknowledged.

The reader will recognize the influence of ancient Chinese philosophy and Buddhist principles throughout the book. The Confucian principle of dual responsibility in relationships, the Chinese concept of the "Mandate from Heaven" and the Buddha's path to enlightenment grounded in doing what is correct or "right," have been wedded together to create a relatively easy to comprehend framework for individuals to strive towards Humanity-at-its-Best. A debt of gratitude is owed to those ancients who produced such wisdom.

Issaac Newton once commented that the reason he was able to discern difficult mathematical and scientific problems was because he was able to

"Stand on the shoulders of giants." I too, owe the same debt of gratitude. The "giants" whose wisdom I have borrowed, have been or are, inhabitants of cultures from around the world. I hope that the reader will discover, as I have, that not only is wisdom universal, but also that no culture has ever had a monopoly on it. There have been many sages in many societies that have provided guidelines for the members of their communities to seek wisdom through pursuing a life of virtue: from the Buddha's Eightfold Path, to the Twelve Virtues of the Lakota, to the "Beatitudes" of Jesus. Their collective wisdom will serve as the backdrop for learning how to live a life based on honor and integrity.

A quick note to the reader. The structure of the book is to highlight the "relationships" in human society that need to be developed and maintained and the "tools" that are used to achieve a harmonious relationship with the world around us. Located below each "relationship" and "tool" are several quotes that support the important role each plays in the quest for Humanity-at-its-Best. These quotes are taken from people who have lived throughout different periods of our history and in different parts of our planet. The quotes, from a diverse collection of cultures, demonstrate the universality of the traits that comprise the canon used in the daily search for achieving Humanity-at-its-Best. When reading and meditating on the quotes, the reader should focus on the meaning of the words and not any personal shortcomings that the author possessed during his/her lifetime. This is vital as no person who has ever lived has been without fault. Political, religious, and social ideologies, as well as prejudices, should be discarded when trying to contemplate the meaning of each quote. It is my hope that the reader will discover through the quotes that the struggle to discover an ethical way of living has been universally sought for and has been a constant throughout human history.

Humanity-At-Its-Best
A Truth Seeker's Guide to Living a Principled Life

"The Need"

One cannot live in modern society and not be aware of the many problems which plague it. The media illuminates us to the latest in terrorist attacks, unending warfare, criminal acts, natural disasters, health risks, and social institutions that fail to meet the needs of citizens. Living in the present has its challenges. Each day presents new problems which seem to get more difficult as they accumulate. Change comes so quickly that many people feel an overwhelming sense of helplessness. Patterns of familiarity are uprooted and quickly replaced. A person's moral compass can find itself with no direction. Despair, anger, and anxiety begin to take root in people's minds and fester into apathy or hopelessness.

The present difficulties have created a nostalgic desire to go back to the good old days when things were not as bad. But were they? Upon close inspection, the student of history will find that the tribulations that we in the present face have been faced by our ancestors as well. Wars, plagues, natural disasters, corruption, and criminal acts have always heavily impacted society. In each generation there is stress put on the social fabric that binds society together. This stress forces each age to ask the same questions: What is truth? What is justice? How should a person live his/her life? How can society meet the varied needs of all its citizens?

If there is a difference between our age and those that have come before, it is only in the speed at which change occurs. It would seem the world needs time to catch its breath. Collectively, we need to pause and reflect, to evaluate our behaviors, institutions, and cultural norms, and to see what areas are in need of repair and improvement. From such discernment, can we then as a society be ready to act.

And act we must. Globally, people are recognizing the precarious situation that exists. People are not hopeful for the future. They see the loss of trust in social institutions. Addiction to power and money has fueled a rise in corruption and the unraveling of the social fabric. Environmental destruction and moral decay have led to universal despair. There exists a strong desire for a "roadmap" to follow that leads humanity on a path to repair both the physical world and the spiritual realm that exists in human souls. And that is the purpose of this book: **to provide direction to a harmonious future by using the wisdom of past and present sages as our guiding light**.

Chapter One
"The First Step"

"I would say 'means are after all everything.' As the means so the end. There is no wall of separation between means and end." Mohandas Gandhi, Young India, July 17th, 1924.

Before a discussion of "what" to do can take place, a prior discussion of "how" to do something is necessary. This is a proper starting place for the person striving to become Humanity-at-its-Best, because the "how" of doing something is more important than the "what" is being done. The accepted belief of modern society is that the end justifies the means. This philosophy of life has become popular in our personal and business lives because it seems to offer easy solutions. In focusing on the end, we can achieve quick results, which can then be proudly displayed. But at what cost? In embracing the idea that the end justifies the means, people will employ deceptions, lies, and the threat or actual use of violence. These are not qualities to strive for.

"Means" are the actions used to reach the desired end. Since all responsibility requires action, it is important that the course of action chosen reflects the end in mind. A noble end cannot be reached using non-noble means. Those that believe it are disillusioned by thinking that the truth can be deceived. Deciding to rearrange one's life to focus on the "means" requires discipline, courage, and the ability to make difficult decisions.

Gandhi spent a great deal of time preaching to his fellow countrymen about the virtue of focusing on the means. In his efforts to achieve independence from Great Britain, he constantly demanded of his followers that they use non-violence in their civil disobedience. He discerned that the "how" (non-violence) was more important than the "end" (freedom from British rule). Or to put it another way, Gandhi employed noble means to achieve a noble end. The respect given by the world community for using non-violence when practicing civil disobedience, is in large part due to the focus on means instead of ends. It is also esteemed because of the method used: non-violence. Individuals who are striving to achieve Humanity-at-its-Best should employ non-violent means to achieve a desired end.

What are some ways that we focus on ends instead of means? Think about the many students who decide to cheat on an assignment or test. These students know they are doing something wrong because they worry themselves sick over the thought of getting caught. But students cheat because they focus on the end (a high grade) instead of the means (studying). There are stockholders who make millions of dollars by using illegally acquired knowledge. Professional athletes routinely use drugs to enhance their performance, so that they can then demand a higher paying contract. Our advertisers use blatant deception to sell products. And finally, politicians have long been known to use a variety of tricks, from misrepresenting their opponents, to making promises they have no intention of keeping, to win elections.

There is no honor or self-respect in being "end" driven instead of being "means" driven. Such thinking does nothing to lead individuals to attain something greater. It simply provides a way for people to avoid the consequences of their actions.

"What ends should Humanity-at-its-Best strive for?"

Being focused on the "means" does not mean that there should be no thought given to the end in mind. We focus on the means so that we might arrive at a noble end. That brings up the question of what should people work and strive for? Socrates declared that the main business in life is to seek out and do what is right and to avoid wrongdoing. K'ung Fu-tzu (Confucius) directed his efforts at the development of his pupils to a high moral code. A more modern perspective comes from Mother Teresa who stated that, "We must have a real living determination to reach holiness." All of these perspectives have something in common: they ask adherents to strive for higher ideals. These higher ideals are: the establishment of justice and living in a state of harmony. Those individuals who believe in God will find that the pursuit of justice and harmony will help them to divine God's will. Those who do not believe in an omnipotent God will simply find that justice and harmony are the best goals to pursue in order to peacefully coexist with the rest of humanity. When people seek to support goals, causes, or programs, they must ask themselves if these ends seek to achieve a higher ideal. A noble end does not debase humanity, it uplifts it.

"How to Recognize a Person Practicing Humanity-at-its-Best"

There is no shortage of individuals today claiming to be of high moral character. And yet, this is in contrast to the perception of the general public that there is a severe shortage of upright individuals. What then, are the traits that we should look for in ourselves, as well as others, so that we can recognize Humanity-at-its-Best? Individuals seeking a higher ideal have in common the characteristics of self-sacrifice, selflessness, diligence, and compassion for humanity.

The Chinese sage K'ung Fu-tzu (Confucius) stressed to his students the importance of maintaining proper relationships. Those practicing Humanity-at-its-Best should strive to do the same. What are the relationships that should be maintained? They are: 1) our relationship to humanity, 2) our relationship to community, 3) our relationship to the environment, 4) our relationship to family, 5) our relationship to work, 6) our relationship to government, and finally, 7) our relationship to the unknown. To maintain these relationships a person striving for Humanity-at-its-Best has an assortment of tools to use as a way of staying "means" focused. These tools will strengthen the will of aspirants and provide courage to make even the most difficult of decisions.

"The First Tool: Empathy"

Empathy is the greatest gift that mankind possesses. The ability to step out of one's own self and to try to imagine the experiences and feelings of another is a powerful force. From empathy springs forth all other qualities that make our species an evolutionary marvel. Our ability to love, offer compassion, seek justice, and sacrifice our personal safety all stem from our ability to empathize with others.

Although there are some higher order animals that have demonstrated some signs of being empathetic, none have made it such an integral part of their existence as humans have. Empathy seems to be the one quality above all others that separates humans from other animals. Empathy is a human quality that is not limited to biological kin. People empathize with other people who do not belong to their clan, tribe, or race. Nor is time a factor. Individuals will weep for people who have been dead for hundreds or thousands of years. Our concern for posterity can be seen as the ability to empathize with those yet to be born. Mankind's ability to empathize is not limited to members of its own kind. People empathize with plants and animals of every sort. Empathy is at the root of all that is good.

If empathy is present in all that is good, then it is also absent in base and evil actions. A murderer can only take the life of another person because they do not possess the ability to empathize with their victim. People who misuse the power they possess do not feel empathy for the individuals who they treat unjustly. Under the skin of every evil action lies an absence of empathy. Thus, every person seeking Humanity-at-its-Best will strive to increase their ability to be empathetic. In every dealing with other living beings, we need to project ourselves into that being and to seek to understand it from a different perspective than our own. This does not mean an abandonment of individual principles. Empathy instead requires the exploration of other possibilities.

Empathy is related to its close sister: compassion. Empathy is the subject and compassion is the verb. Compassion is the action one takes after empathizing with another. Compassion is the outward, noticeable display of empathy. Empathy and compassion are both concerned with the elimination of the suffering of others. Empathy and compassion allow us to bond and form a communion with people, animals, and nature. To act on one's empathy is to be compassionate. Empathy is one of the central traits of a person striving for Humanity-at-its-Best.

Cross-Cultural Quotes in Support of Empathy

Humanity's collective mission in the cosmos lies in the practice of compassion." Dalsaku Ikeda, Japanese philosopher

"Empathy is seeing with the eyes of another, listening with the ears of another and feeling with the heart of another." – Alfred Adler

"The purpose of human life is to serve, and to show compassion and the will to help others." – Albert Schweitzer

"Empathy may be the single most important quality that must be nurtured to give peace a fighting chance." – Arundhati Ray

"We have to teach empathy as we do literacy." – Bill Drayton

Do not judge your neighbor until you walk two moons in his moccasins. *-American Indian Proverb, Cheyenne*

Empathy is putting yourself in another's shoes to find out what exactly that person is feeling or going through at the given time. It basically refers to being at a common wavelength with someone." - Deepa Kodikal

Empathy is the only human superpower-it can shrink distance, cut through social and power hierarchies, transcend differences, and provoke political and social change. — Elizabeth Thomas

" I told you once that I was searching for the nature of Evil. I think I've come close to defining it. A lack of empathy. It's one characteristic that connects all the defendants. A genuine incapacity to feel with their fellow man. Evil I think, is the absence of empathy. "Gustav M. Gilbert From movie - Nuremberg (2000) Nazi Leaders on trial

"A human being is a part of the whole, called by us 'Universe,' a part limited in time and space. He experiences himself, his thoughts and feelings as something separated from the rest—a kind of optical delusion of his consciousness. This delusion is a kind of prison for us, restricting us to our personal desires and to affection for a few persons nearest to us. **Our task must be to free ourselves from this prison by widening our circle of compassion to embrace all living creatures and the whole nature in its beauty.** Nobody is able to achieve this completely, but the striving for such achievement is in itself a part of the liberation and a foundation for inner security."- Albert Einstein

"The Second Tool: Non-violence"

Since the use of non-violence has been discussed earlier, it would only be appropriate to examine it as a tool used to reach an end. The twentieth century saw an increase in the use of non-violence as a method for social change. Leaders of non-violent protests, such as Gandhi and Martin Luther King Jr., are generally recognized around the world as examples of Humanity-at-its-Best. This is due in large part because of how they achieved their goals. Non-violence requires the ability to use courage, integrity, and compassion in every action. Non-violence is the blueprint in the construction of an end.

One reason why non-violence has achieved success is because it relies on persuasion instead of coercion. The practitioner of non-violence acts on individual convictions with the hope that it will engage others in moral reflection. Non-violence appeals to the noble, rather than the savage side of man.

Non-violence asks that a person see the broader picture. It requires compassion for humanity, other animals, and nature. It makes one more empathetic. This empathy allows a person to feel a sense of belonging with other members of the community. A sense of belonging instills a desire to see the whole community prosper. When everyone prospers an environment of trust is established. A climate of trust leads to a willingness to work together. When a community works together, conflicts can be resolved. A community that can work together to reduce conflicts is a community where justice and harmony thrive. Such is the power of non-violence.

Living a life of non-violence requires an individual to cultivate the capacity for self-sacrifice. It requires suffering through hardships. But there is a payoff. There is an inner joy that can be experienced from voluntarily bearing such burdens, as well as the satisfaction from attempting to demonstrate the value of nonviolent action to another community member. A person striving for Humanity-at-its-Best should therefore strive to lead a life of non-violence. All of mankind's endeavors to make a positive change in the world are doomed to failure if we do not put into practice the daily use of non-violence.

The adoption of non-violence by those seeking Humanity-at-its-Best will bring the adherent to experience an inner peace. That peace will then be extended to other relationships between family, friends, strangers, other nations, and the environment. Non-violence is an essential tool to be used by those seeking Humanity-at-its-Best in the reduction of violence between individuals, groups, and nations.

Additional benefits from adopting non-violence as a personal philosophy are improved relations with those closest to you. Taking an oath to live non-violently means children should not fear beatings from their parents, those dating or married have less fear of abuse from their partners and spouses, and community members can feel safe in their persons and property.

Cross-Cultural Quotes in Support of Non-Violence

Violence just hurts those who are already hurt… Instead of exposing the brutality of the oppressor, it justifies it. - Cesar Chavez

Should anyone confront you with violence, you should try and repel it with peacefulness, whereby he who is your enemy will become your friend. - Holy Qur'an (41:34)

"We adopt the means of nonviolence because our end is a community at peace with itself. We will try to persuade with our words, but if our words fail, we will try to persuade with our acts." - Martin Luther King Jr.

"Nonviolence is the greatest force at the disposal of mankind. It is mightier than the mightiest weapon of destruction devised by the ingenuity of man." - Mahatma Gandhi

He who has renounced all violence towards all living beings, weak or strong, who neither kills nor causes others to kill- him I do call a holy man. Only by nonviolence is excellence achieved. - Gautama Buddha

It is no longer good enough to cry peace, we must act peace, live peace and live in peace. – Leon Shenandoah Onondaga chief

The improvement of life was only accomplished to the extent to which it was based on a change of consciousness, that is, to the extent to which the law of violence was replaced in men's consciousness by the law of love. - Leo Tolstoy

Jesus: "You have heard that it was said, 'An eye for an eye and a tooth for a tooth.' But I say to you, do not resist the one who is evil. But if anyone slaps you on the right cheek, turn to him the other also." - Matthew 5:38 - 39

Violence never settles anything right: apart from injuring your own soul, it injures the best cause. It lingers on long after the object of hate has disappeared from the scene to plague the lives of those who have employed it against their foes. - Obafemi Awolowo

"The Third Tool: Integrity"

Integrity is a quality that many strive for, but few achieve. But what is integrity? When we look at people in history who are deemed to have lived an integral life (Socrates, Confucius, Jesus, the Buddha, Gandhi) we seem to think we know what it means. These people advocated leading a life based on certain principles, principles that they tried very hard to put into practice.

People striving to lead an integral life are self-aware that they are striving to reach lofty principles. Furthermore, so are their contemporaries. This recognition of effort permits us to admire and respect such people of integrity. But how did someone such as Martin Luther King Jr. use integrity to reach for lofty ideals? He did so by acting on three characteristics of integrity as espoused by Stephen Carter in his book, Integrity. His first characteristic of integrity is the step of discerning what is right and wrong. This involves work. It might mean long, serious reflection. It might mean conducting research, or reading numerous books, or interviewing many people. But all effort must contain moral reflection. Christ's time spent in the desert, or the Buddha's time spent under the Lotus tree are examples of exerting an effort to discover what is the right path towards truth. The second characteristic of integrity according to Carter is acting on your discernment, even at personal cost. Socrates, acting on his beliefs, chose to forfeit his life, rather than his integrity. In the modern era, those who use civil disobedience in defense of their beliefs, from the Civil Rights protesters in America during the 1960's to anti-war protestors today, have earned the public's respect precisely because they put their lives in danger. Finally, Carter's third principle of integrity is to publicly state that your actions are based on your discernment of what is right and wrong. There is little room for secrecy in leading an integral life. The ability to stand up for what we believe, to have courage in our convictions, is essential to instill in people a sense of trust. Those seeking Humanity-at-its-Best should make time for serious reflection, be open about their views, and show courage by publicly acting on their beliefs.

Cross-Cultural Quotes in Support of Integrity

"One of the truest tests of integrity is its blunt refusal to be compromised." - Chinua Achebe
"The greatness of a man is not in how much wealth he acquires, but in his integrity and his ability to affect those around him positively." - Bob Marley
"The integrity of men is to be measured by their conduct, not by their professions." - Junius
"I prefer to be true to myself, even at the hazard of incurring the ridicule of others, rather than to be false, and to incur my own abhorrence." - Frederick Douglass
"Integrity is doing the right thing, even when no one is watching." - C.S. Lewis
"Integrity is making sure that the things you say and the things you do are in alignment." - Katrina Mayer
"Integrity is the seed for achievement. It is the principle that never fails." Earl Nightingale
"Those who conduct themselves with morality, integrity and consistency need not fear the forces of inhumanity and cruelty." - Nelson Mandella

"The Fourth Tool: Honor"

Honor is a quality that has always been prized by various cultures throughout history. Honor brings up images of the Age of Chivalry in European history and the Japanese Samurai soldier in feudal Japan. Honor is a quality that many organizations try to create and then impose on their members. Such is the case in military units, political organizations, and other societal groups. This type of honor can be beneficial to both the individual and the group. But it is not the most desirable type of honor.

The highest and most difficult form of honor is that which is self-imposed. When honor moves inward then it brings with it the element of self-respect. This is important, for self-respect is where individual honor is to be found. This is where the inner voice holds court and pronounces judgements on beliefs and behaviors. It is this type of honor that cannot be taken away, only given.

Honor is not without its problems. People place their honor in the most absurd places. Witness the supposed honor of the German and Japanese military in World War II or what passes for honor in political offices today. To what/who do we pledge our honor to? Honor is a part of ourselves that must be self-examined on a daily basis. We must be constantly vigil in monitoring what actions and beliefs we consider honorable. When a course of action is being debated, we must ask ourselves, is it nonviolent? Means driven? Will our integrity be compromised? Is compassion and empathy present? A person's code of honor is something that can be modified and changed after reflection and discernment.

What makes honor appealing to people is that it consists of a list of do's and don'ts. Possessing a code of honor can help in decision making. It guides an individual to the right course of action. Correct actions are those that move toward virtue and away from vice. Honor that is carefully cultivated, monitored and revised, when necessary, is vital in attaining "Humanity-at-its-Best."

Cross-Cultural Quotes in Support of Honor

"Rather fail with honor, than succeed by fraud." - Sophocles

"Who sows virtue, reaps honor." - Leonardo de Vinci

"Nobility of soul is more honorable than nobility of birth." - Dutch proverb

"Honorable is the person who is aware of his power, yet refrains from inflicting bad things onto others." - Egyptian Proverb

"Honor is the reward of virtue." - Cicero

"Honor is the moral conscience of the great." - Sir William D'Avenant

"Honor is self-esteem made visible in action." - Ayn Rand

"My honor is dearer to me than my life." – Cervantes

"I maintain that men and women are happy if they are honorable and upright, but miserable if they are vicious and wicked." - Socrates

"We will be known forever by the tracks we leave." - Dakota proverb

"The Fifth Tool: Duty"

Duty is a concept that has seen its importance rise and fall with the annals of history. In previous ages duty was a call to act in a prescribed, traditional way. But in the twentieth century, duty has been subverted by various organizations, including the nation state, to get individuals to act in ways that help meet the organization's needs. Many of these "calls to duty" have led to dishonorable actions. Duty has a very close relationship to integrity. It requires a person to spend time reflecting on the urge to respond. A person seeking to be Humanity-at-its-Best should always be asking the questions, "what principle should I act on?" "What action should I take in observance of duty?"

One of duty's main features is its reliance on action. Unlike its cousin Rights, duty is not passive. It does not make demands and ask for action from someone else. Duty demands individual action, an account of responsibility. The action taken is not dependent on the action of others. It is born out of the discernment of principles. One feels an inner "compulsion" to act. To not act would be to abandon the principles that one cherishes. Outside the personal benefits to performing a duty, there are societal benefits as well. The act of carrying out one's duty establishes a sense of trust with other members of the community. When you have made public your beliefs, and your commitment to uphold those beliefs, then the community can invest its trust, which will go a long way in establishing peaceful living conditions among its members.

The best way to find yourself is to lose yourself in the service of others. - Mahatma Gandhi

To do one's duty is to eat the prized fruit of honor. - Nigerian Proverb

A kingdom's strength is in mutual honor. - Bantu Proverb

In doing what we ought we deserve no praise, because it is our duty. - St. Augustine

I think the first duty of society is justice. - Alexander Hamilton

The most beautiful things in the universe are the starry heavens above us and the feeling of duty within us. - Indian Proverb

It is an achievement for a man to do his duty on earth irrespective of the consequences. - Nelson Mandella

As birds are made to fly and rivers to run, so the soul to follow duty. - Ramayana

Duty is a very personal thing. It is what comes from knowing the need to take action and not just a need to urge others to do something. - Mother Theresa

The sense of duty is the fountain of human rights. - William Ellery Channing

"The Sixth Tool: Self-Discipline"

Self-discipline is the constant monitoring process a person uses to regulate behavior. There are many times when we are tempted to engage in a dishonorable act. But self-discipline restrains the urge. It calls into our consciousness the reasons why we should or should not act. Having then made a decision, it ushers in the will to act upon conviction.

Many of the great people of history have commented on the importance of self-discipline in their lives. Control over urges and desires allows a person to think and act more clearly. It reduces the destructive forces that can prohibit us from acting with honor and integrity. Daily exercises, such as yoga, fasts, prayer, and meditation have all been used by those seeking Humanity-At-Its-Best to increase one's self-discipline.

As is always the case, it is important to reflect on what one should be disciplined about. There are people who have disciplined themselves to walk down a busy urban street and not notice those looking for assistance. Or others who have disciplined themselves to commit violent acts. The person seeking Humanity-At-Its-Best seeks instead to be disciplined in thinking empathetically and acting compassionately. Self-discipline allows a person to be consistent in their actions which leads to a reputation for integrity. The repetition of self-discipline will be codified into one's personal honor.

Cross-Cultural Quotes in Support of Self-Discipline

He who lives without discipline dies without honor. - Icelandic Proverb

"A disciplined mind leads to happiness, and an undisciplined mind leads to suffering." – Dalai Lama

"Most powerful is he who has himself in his own power." – Seneca

"I count him braver who overcomes his desires than him who conquers his enemies; for the hardest victory is over self." – Aristotle

"It is better to conquer self than to win a thousand battles." – Buddha

The devoted and disciplined person who controls his mind will attain tranquility and oneness. - Bhagavad Gita

"Discipline yourself and others won't need to." - John Wooden

"He who controls others may be powerful, but he who has mastered himself is mightier still." - Lao Tzu

"For the moment all discipline seems painful rather than pleasant, but later it yields the peaceful fruit of righteousness to those who have been trained by it." - Hebrews 12:11

'The strong man is not the one who knocks people down; the truly strong man is the one who can control himself in anger." - The Prophet Mohammed

"The Seventh Tool: Moderation"

Moderation is a by-product of the first six tools. By living a life of reflection, by trying to be empathetic in every situation, a person is able to step outside of their local habitat and begin to view the world more globally. The search for justice, for truth, removes the constraints of time, location, citizenship, tribe, and family. Passionate arguments from various groups, all calling on you to view events from their perspective, do not cause the person striving for Humanity-At-Its-Best to lose his/her ability to be objective. Since all perspectives are to be examined, it becomes difficult to take extremist positions.

There are many examples in history where the benefits of moderation have been extolled and the avoidance of extremes emphasized. After living a life of a prince and then as a hermit, Buddha preached a doctrine called the Middle Way, which asks adherents to avoid the extremes of pleasure seeking and rejection of everything worldly. Aristotle had his Golden Mean. Each side of an extreme carries with it traits which can obscure the solution to a problem or prevent the acquisition of knowledge. Taking the middle road is not the position of cowards, as some people think, but rather the position of someone who has spent time reflecting on issues and trying to have the vantage point of all perspectives.

Cross-Cultural Quotes in Support of Moderation

Even nectar is poison if taken to excess. - Hindu proverb
In all circumstances they should conduct themselves with moderation. - Baha'u'llah, Lights of Guidance
Moderation is the silken string running through the pearl chain of all virtues. - Joseph Hall
"Moderation is a wiser policy than zealotry" - Christopher Paolini, Brisingr
"If one oversteps the bounds of moderation, the greatest pleasures cease to please." - Epictetus
To go beyond the bounds of moderation is to outrage humanity. The greatness of the human soul is shown by knowing how to keep within proper bounds. There are two equally dangerous extremes- to shut reason out, and not to let nothing in." - Blaise Pascal
Temperance is moderation in the things that are good and total abstinence from the things that are

foul." - Frances E. Willard

"The world has enough for everyone's need, but not enough for everyone's greed."- Gandhi

"Whatsoever passeth beyond the limits of moderation will cease to exert a beneficial influence." — Baha'u'llah, Baha'i prophet

"The Eighth Tool: A Sense of Humor"

It might seem out of place to include a sense of humor as a necessary tool in developing a person to his or her full potential. But without it, a person might not be able to carry out the hard work that striving to be an example of Humanity-At-Its-Best entails. One could not find the joy in living without a sense of humor. Gandhi once said, "If I had no sense of humor, I should long ago have committed suicide." As a matter of survival, we need a sense of humor to overcome life's many obstacles, daily tribulations, and our own failures.

And yet, there is a connection between moderation and a sense of humor. Taking life too seriously can lead a person to take extremist positions. Focusing on a single cause or issue can sap a person's ability to notice anything else. Zealots are recognizable by the way they get upset when their passion is not shared by others. They divide the world into "us" and "them" and lose the sense of interconnectedness that we share with others. These people lose the ability to poke fun at themselves or their cause. Without moderation, a person becomes single minded and unbalanced. Without humor, a person loses their humanity. Expressing joy in all its forms- laughing, singing, dancing- should be encouraged.

Cross-Cultural Quotes in Support of Humor

"No matter what happens, somebody will find a way to take it too seriously." - Dave Barry

Humor is mankind's greatest blessing. - Mark Twain

If I had no sense of humor, I would long ago have committed suicide. - Mahatma Gandhi

There is a thin line that separates laughter and pain, comedy and tragedy, humor and hurt. - Erma Bombeck

The duty of comedy is to correct men by amusing them. - Moliere

Humor is the weapon of unarmed people: it helps people who are oppressed to smile at the situation that pains them. - Simon Wiesenthal

Humor is one of the best ingredients of survival. - Aung San Suu Kyi

This I conceive to be the chemical function of humor: to change the character of our thought. - Lin Yutang

When we are dealing with death we are constantly being dragged down by the event: Humor diverts our attention and lifts our sagging spirits. - Allen Klein

The tools I have outlined above are not unique. Many people from many cultures have for centuries expounded their virtue. I have done nothing more than to capsulize and string together their significance. The question remains: how can these tools be put to use? In the next section I will examine how these tools can be used in the various relationships which bind our lives together.

Chapter Two
"The First Relationship: Achieving a Harmonious Relationship with Humanity"

Humanity is a club that all people can claim membership in. Yet, each day seems to bring new news on how we are committing "crimes against humanity." I think Jesus was asking us to love humanity when he implored us to love strangers and enemies as well as those that we know. In general terms, we should see people to be like ourselves, full of admirable qualities as well as faults. In each of us exists the possibility to lead lives of either virtue or vise. It is the duty of the person seeking Humanity-at-Its-Best to seek the life of virtue and to instill the desire to become virtuous in others. This can be done most effectively through teaching, instead of preaching.

It is important to note the difference between preaching and teaching. Preaching begets a "Holier than thou" attitude, where the speaker monopolizes the discussion and creates an "I" and "You" environment, where "I" knows what is right, and "You" should listen. Teaching on the other hand, focuses on a collaborative effort between the speaker and the audience. The teacher will use his/her knowledge to begin a discussion, and if successful, will bring out many varied opinions. Through such an open discussion, both the teacher and the audience are in a position to increase their enlightenment. A dialectic (both-sided inquiry and exchange of ideas) should be the foundation of truth seeking and understanding. Gandhi developed 'Satyagraha' (Hindi 'truth-search') in his attempt to engage and reform those participating in violent or unjust acts. Those of us living in modern times must relearn the ancient ritual of engaging in a public dialogue where we listen and speak to each other and where the exchange of ideas and positions is disseminated to the general public for consideration and debate.

The most important way to teach about living a life of integrity and honor is to use your life as an example. As the old saying goes, "Actions speak louder than words." Such a life will provide inspiration to others in the community. Since both successes and failures are equally important, it is necessary that a person striving for Humanity-at-its-Best attempt to lead as open a life as possible and to avoid secrecy.

Each person who desires to achieve Humanity-at-its-Best should become a student of human society. This entails a serious inquiry into a variety of subjects such as literature, history, philosophy, science, sociology, psychology, political science, and economics, among others. This means not just studying thinkers from one's own society but discovering the richness of thought found in other cultures. Such an endeavor should protect against the adoption of prejudices, stereotypes, and the assimilation of propaganda.

One of the goals of seeking Humanity-at-its-Best is to use the seeking of truth to eliminate the illusions others try to create for us, as well as to eliminate the delusions we create for ourselves.

For a person seeking Humanity-at-its-Best there should be a striving to be more inclusive and expand the number of people included in your "in-group" and a reduction of those considered in the "out-group." In short- more "us" and less "them." This can be accomplished by recognizing through contemplation, study, and life experiences that all people mourn the loss of a loved one, celebrate the birth of a child, look forward to the end of a workday, get frustrated with the obstacles that life throws at us, relish the taste of a favorite meal, and seek out companionship. The wonders, joys, and sorrows of life bind all people. Those seeking Humanity-at-its-Best should focus on similarities amongst people, and not differences.

Cross-Cultural Quotes in Support of Achieving a
Harmonious Relationship with Humanity

Just as a mother would protect her only child with her life, even so let one cultivate a boundless love towards all beings. - Buddha

"An individual has not started living until he can rise above the narrow confines of his individualistic concerns to the broader concerns of all humanity." - Martin Luther King, Jr.

"Be certain that you do not die without having done something wonderful for humanity."

-Maya Angelou

"In recognizing the humanity of our fellow beings, we pay ourselves the highest tribute."

-Thurgood Marshall

"The sole meaning of life is to serve humanity."- Leo Tolstoy

"You cannot hope to build a better world without improving the individuals. To that end, each of us must work for his own improvement and, at the same time, share a general responsibility for all humanity, our particular duty being to aid those to whom we think we can be most useful."- Marie Curie

"My humanity is bound up in yours, for we can only be human together." - Desmond Tutu

"Act in such a way that you treat humanity, whether in your own person or in the person of any other, never merely as a means to an end, but always at the same time as an end."- Immanuel Kant

"I'm for truth, no matter who tells it. I'm for justice, no matter who it is for or against. I'm a human being, first and foremost, and as such I'm for whoever and whatever benefits humanity as a whole."- Malcolm X

How wonderful it is that nobody need wait a single moment before starting to improve the world. - Anne Frank, The Diary of a Young Girl

"If you want to go fast, go alone; if you want to go far, go together." - African Proverb

"The Second Relationship: Achieving a Harmonious Relationship with Your Local Community"

Just as a tree spreads its roots throughout the forest floor, so too should a person seeking Humanity-at-its-Best spread his/her roots throughout the community that they reside in. How can a person striving for Humanity-at-its-Best live in harmony with fellow community members? Such a person should live in accordance with the list below:

1)Secure a residence that is geographically near to one's place of occupation.

2)Support local businesses by purchasing as many daily needs as possible from those who live near you.

3)Attend community events to support your locality and to get to know your neighbors.

4)Engage in local events such as school board meetings, town hall meetings, serving on juries, and non-violent protests against injustice.

Focusing on the local community is logical. Most of the encounters a person has in a given week will be with people from the local community- coworkers, teachers, owners of shops and restaurants. If local relationships are in harmony, then that harmony can be shared with other communities practicing Humanity-at-its-Best, producing a contagion that spreads across the globe. Creating strong ties to the local community will also be helpful in times of crisis, such as natural disasters, responding to climate and environmental change, and in the prevention and ending of civil strife.

Those striving for Humanity-at-its-Best should live within the local community of their neighbors, co-workers, and fellow citizens and not seek to establish separate residential dwellings with only like-minded thinkers. This is necessary to remove suspicion from fellow community members that those seeking Humanity-at-its- Best are engaged in some form of illegal or unethical behavior and to instead create bonds and friendships that will ensure learning from each other and working jointly to reduce the suffering inflicted on community members because of the absence of justice.

Cross-Cultural Quotes in Support of Your Local Community

"There is no power for change greater than a community discovering what it cares about." – Margaret J. Wheatley

"The greatness of a community is most accurately measured by the compassionate actions of its members." – Coretta Scott King

"Alone, we can do so little; together, we can do so much" – Helen Keller

"I am of the opinion that my life belongs to the whole community and as long as I live, it is my privilege to do for it whatever I can. I want to be thoroughly used up when I die, for the harder I work the more I live." – George Bernard Shaw

"The power of community to create health is far greater than any physician, clinic or hospital." – Mark Hyman

"We were born to unite with our fellow men, and to join in community with the human race." – Cicero

We have all known the long loneliness and we have learned that the only solution is love and that love comes with community." – Dorothy Day

He who masters the power formed by a group of people working together has within his grasp one of the greatest powers known to man." – Idowu Koyenikan

A true community is not just about being geographically close to someone or part of the same social web network. It's about feeling connected and responsible for what happens. Humanity is our ultimate community, and everyone plays a crucial role." – Yehuda Berg

"Service is the rent we pay for living, the anchor to our humanity." – Oneida Proverb

"The Third Relationship: Achieving a Harmonious Relationship with the Environment"

The earth is the ancestral home to all species. Maintaining life- all life- is of paramount importance to the person striving for Humanity-at-its-Best. The volume of books written about how humanity is destroying the ability of life to be sustained on the Earth could fill a library. It could be argued that there is no more important relationship to maintain than that of maintaining a healthy and thriving environment since if the Earth becomes inhabitable, the other relationships become meaningless.

So, what steps can be taken to restore the earth to a more pristine and self-sustaining planet? Those pursuing Humanity-at-its-Best should strive to achieve the recommendations below.

The first is to reestablish the truism that humans are part of the ecosystem on this planet and not separate from it. This means that for the human species to thrive, the planet needs to thrive. A rethinking of the hierarchy of life needs to occur. Humans are subservient to the needs of the planet, not the other way around.

Humanity needs to stop exploiting nature and learn to live in harmony with it. To live in harmony with nature is to recognize that all living things are interconnected. The wisdom of interconnectedness prevents those seeking Humanity-at-its-Best from the hubris that humans can thrive without the existence of all the other species that populate our wonderful planet. Those striving for Humanity-at-its-Best should recognize that all species have a right to exist for their own sake- not for the pleasure or profit of homo sapiens. To live in harmony with nature means to allow nature to follow its cycles- of the rebirth of life following death, of spring following winter, and of evolutionary change from continuity.

Vegetarianism. Our species, like all others, needs to consume energy to survive. A good argument can be made that the consumption of meat, with its stockpile of protein, allowed our brains to develop and with it our intelligence to expand. And although we may still need to consume protein to thrive, we do not need the source to be from other animal species. Our intelligence has allowed our species to evolve to the more advanced qualities of empathy and compassion. Which means we no longer need to view other animal species as a source of food. We can now acquire protein from plant sources. As a species, we should be moving away from eating meat and towards vegetarianism first. Then from vegetarianism to veganism. It should be recognized that this process will occur at different speeds and in different ways around the world, due to cultural factors, geographic location (for example groups living in the Arctic region who have limited access to plant food) and social factors (poor people who need to eat whatever is available to survive). Those seeking Humanity-at-its-Best should attempt to become vegetarians or vegans with the understanding that the same constraints that face groups described above (cultural, geographic, and social) will also be faced by individuals. Attempts should also be made to investigate the source of food consumed. For example, it is less harmful to eat an egg from a local farmer who allows chickens to roam around cage-free, than to consume an egg from a factory farm. It is better to eat food that is truly organic, grown without pesticides and herbicides, than the chemically contaminated food grown by corporations. If living conditions allow for it, those striving for Humanity-at-its-Best should try to grow some of their own food so they can create a connection with their ancestors, as well as with the earth itself.

Incorporating a vegetarian or vegan diet into one's life employs two of the tools of Humanity-at-its-Best (non-violence) and (empathy) in the service of living in harmony with nature.

Ending business externalities. The current global, capitalist system is designed so that businesses can avoid paying for the true cost of producing goods that have an undesirable effect on the environment. Externalities refer to a cost or benefit that arises from an economic transaction and that falls on people who may or may not have participated in the transaction. For example, if a factory dumps toxic waste into a river making it dangerous to swim, it imposes an external cost on people who enjoy swimming. When the factory dumped the waste into the river, they did not take the views of those who enjoy swimming into account. Most of the environmental problems that we face today, such as global warming, water and air pollution, are the result of these harmful externalities. The end result of businesses externalizing their environmental costs are the polluted air and water, the extinction of a large number of species, and a future, unlivable planet. Businesses must be forced to pay for the full cost of producing their goods, and consumers must be made aware of their role in externalizing negative costs on the environment.

Simple living. As the number of humans increases, the stress on the environment increases as well. The earth cannot sustain unlimited, continued growth. There is no future for life on the planet if humanity continues to use resources at current levels. There is no path to coexistence and harmony with nature where the dominant world economic system emphasizes unlimited growth on a planet with finite resources. This means that humanity must embrace the idea to "live simply, so others may simply live." The term "others" refers to not only people, but all species, all life on the planet. Simple living utilizes the tool of "moderation" to achieve its goal.

Establishing a love for nature as a unifying world philosophy. For humans to live in harmony with nature, there needs to be established a reverence and awe for the planet. This reverence can be acquired through instruction about, and a personal connection with, nature beginning at an early age and continuing throughout one's life. Children should be encouraged to play outside, to run through the meadows, to swim in its lakes and rivers, to climb its hills, and to worship its beauty. These activities should not be forgotten and left in childhood. They should be carefully nurtured throughout adulthood. Those seeking Humanity-at-its Best should establish regular rituals to honor nature by helping restore that which has been destroyed, as well as to spend time in nature in order to better appreciate its wonder and beauty.

Protecting endangered species, restoring habitat, and creating a new paradise should be a way to unify our species to do something constructive instead of destructive. If we need a higher purpose to serve, or a new deity to prostrate ourselves to, then let it be to Gaia, or any of its other ancient manifestations (Pachamama, Prithvi, or the Spider Grandmother of Southwest Native American cultures.) In ancient Greek mythology, the giant Antaeus, whose mother was Ge (the Earth), gained renewed strength every time he came into contact with the ground. Each of us must find in ourselves that same powerful connection to the earth.

Cross-Cultural Quotes in Support of a Harmonious Relationship with the Environment

The North American Lakota term, *Mitákuye Oyás'in* (all our relations) recognizes this fundamental kinship among all beings.

Ute Prayer: Treat the earth well. It was not given to you by your parents, it was loaned to you by your children. We do not inherit the Earth from our Ancestors; we borrow it from our Children.

"The Holy Land is everywhere." - *Black Elk*

We are not independent but interdependent. - Gautama Buddha

"Preserve and cherish the pale blue dot, the only home we've ever known." - Carl Sagen

"Look at a tree, a flower, a plant. Let your awareness rest upon it. How still they are, how deeply rooted in Being. Allow nature to teach you stillness." —Eckhart Tolle

"No one comes from the earth like grass. We come like trees. We all have roots." —Maya Angelou

"Look after the land and the land will look after

you, destroy the land and it will destroy you." —
Aboriginal Proverb

"The earth does not belong to us; we belong to the earth." - Chief Seattle

"Those who contemplate the beauty of the earth find reserves of strength that will endure as long as life lasts." - Rachel Carson

"Mother Earth, may whatever I dig from you grow back again quickly, and may we not injure you by our labour." —Atharva Veda

"The Fourth Relationship: Achieving a Harmonious Relationship with Family"

The family unit has been the basis for the social organization of humans for thousands of years. It has been the source of great comfort, as well as great sorrow. For countless millennia parents have been tasked by human society with the nurturing and development of children. Because of an imbalance in power in the structure of the family, relationships between family members can be problematic and create disharmony. To improve relationships and to achieve harmony, the Chinese concept of the "Mandate from Heaven" is once again a useful guidance for both parents and children. Paired with the Mandate From Heaven are the tools of empathy, non-violence, duty, honor, and self-discipline.

Parenting has always been the most difficult job. It requires enormous energy, time, and resources to raise children. It is an even more difficult task when dealing with poverty. Society at large offers little in the way of resources and training. Humanity-at-its-Best can be used to help parents and children throughout the life course.

While empathy is necessary at every age, it is most important in the infant and toddler stages. Because young human children are often helpless- but yet inquisitive, they need constant supervision. This requires patience. And that patience comes from empathy and discipline. There is no reason to use violence in administering discipline at any age- but especially when young.

Parents have a duty to provide for the well-being of their children until they have reached the age where they are viewed as legal adults. This duty to assist children should continue into adulthood as long as the child is striving to live a life of empathy, integrity, and honor or suffering from a severe physical or mental disease. If, however, an adult offspring pursues a career focusing on profiting from the exploitation of the poor or vulnerable, engages in criminal activity, or other dishonorable acts, then the parent is released from the duty of continued support. If later the adult child embraces a course of redemption, then the parent has an obligation to forgive and to resume all parental duties.

Relations between siblings and the duty of children to take care of aging parents should be guided by the same sense of duty as described above. As long as siblings and parents are attempting to embrace the principles of Humanity-at-its-Best, then there is a duty to seek harmonious relations with all family members.

The parents of children with special needs should receive extra help and assistance from family members, the community, and the state in the care of raising their children. The physical and emotional demands of providing non-stop care to such children is a task too difficult to bear for most parents.

Parents, siblings, sons and daughters must put in the hard work of earning the respect and support of family members by seeking to live a virtuous life and not harming others. Many people believe that they must maintain family fealty by visiting or inviting to their homes family members who are members in a criminal gang, support dishonorable ideologies such as fascism, or engage in violent or base activities due to the trafficking of illegal drugs. The argument is used that **you** "must support", "must associate", "must love" **me** because I am your sister, son, or father. Such a plea is only valid if there is remorse shown, or if guilt is professed and forgiveness sought. No "accident of birth" can justify and compel individuals to associate with, and care for, family members who willingly engage in the debauchery of their souls. There exists no social custom pressuring individuals to associate with such people if they were **not** members of an individual's family, so none should exist because they are. Adherents should always keep open the option of redemption and forgiveness.

Historically, the family unit has been the place where humans as a species, have socialized and instructed its members on matters related to dating/courtship, marriage, raising children, and sexual relations. It would seem then, that a few words should be devoted to describing how the principles of Humanity-at-its-Best should influence these traditions.

The application of empathy shows that many historical and current practices within the family unit are unjust. Child marriage is a good example. Imagine being in the shoes of a young thirteen-year-old girl who is told without her consent that she is to be wed to someone three to four times her age. Any compassionate person would recoil at the thought of being in such a girl's shoes. The anxiety of being separated from her parents at such a young age, of being required to have sex with an older man, of being made subservient in a strange house is too much to bear for one so young. The principle of non-violence means no forced coercion can be used to force such a young girl into marriage. Integrity requires that no elderly male should make such a request of their community. Any sexual relations between these two could only be described as rape, since the young girl could not or did not, consent to the marriage. Nor is there honor to be found in parents, matchmakers, and community elders agreeing to and sanctioning such an unequal marriage. Instead, there is a duty for all community members to put empathy at the forefront in these types of decisions. In this example of child marriage, the autotomy of the child cannot be ignored. The health and development of her soul becomes paramount.

The above example concerning child marriages can be used as a template for other issues inside the family. Whom a person chooses to have sexual relations with is determined by the principles of Humanity-at-its-Best. Adults should not have sexual relations with children because of the inequality that exists based on age and experience, which means consent cannot be attained- but also because integrity, empathy, honor and duty prohibits it. The same principles should be applied to those who suffer from physical or cognitive disabilities.

Sexual relations between consenting adults should also follow the principles of Humanity-at-its-Best. The principle of non-violence means that rape can never be attempted or justified. No violence may be used against consenting, adult community members engaged in heterosexual, homosexual or lesbian sex. If there is no violence, force or coercion, community members have a duty to respect their fellow community members' privacy in all matters- especially when it comes to sexual relations- as that is a uniquely private matter. It is the duty of everyone seeking Humanity-at-its-Best to honor the privacy of their community member's sexual lives (once again consenting adults with no violence or coercion involved) and not try to force one's individual beliefs about what constitutes acceptable sexual relations onto others.

Those seeking Humanity-at-its-Best should show respect to their ancestors for the actions they chose to provide a fertile present, as well as for the descendants yet born who will tend to the garden of humanity. Filial piety to the past and future is an honorable endeavor.

Finally, the goal of someone striving for Humanity-at-its-Best should be to expand the number of people one considers to be family.

Cross-Cultural Quotes in Support of a Harmonious Relationship with the Family

African proverb: It takes a village to raise a child. Although this phrase has been misinterpreted to mean the interference of "big government" in the raising of children, its meaning is more about how all members of a community have a vested interest in making sure children behave according to social norms and that any adult may get involved in correcting misconduct.

"The key that unlocks is also the key that locks. Honor a child, and he will honor you." - African Proverb

To support mother and father, to cherish wife and child and to have a simple livelihood; this is the good luck. - Buddha

"The golden way is to be friends with the world and to regard the whole human family as one." – Mahatma Gandhi

"The bond that links your true family is not one of blood, but of respect and joy in each other's life." – Richard Bach

"A happy family is but an earlier heaven." – George Bernard Shaw

"There is no doubt that it is around the family and the home that all the greatest virtues… are created, strengthened and maintained." –Winston Churchill

"The ones that matter the most are the children." – Lakota Proverb

"The whole world is one family." - Sun Yat-sen

"Rejoice with your family in the beautiful land of life." – Albert Einstein

"The Fifth Relationship: Achieving a Harmonious Relationship with the World of Work"

Individuals pursuing Humanity-at-its-Best should seek and secure employment that promotes the general health and well-being of the community. It should be acknowledged that this task is more difficult in countries where economic development has not progressed to the point where there are many honorable types of employment beyond low paying, but life sustaining, agricultural work.

It is becoming more difficult under the world capitalist system to find honorable work. The legally created non-human entity called the corporation is unaccountable and is destroying the planet. The corporation, an offspring of capitalism, which was created to assist humanity by mitigating risk, has now morphed into an entity that has enslaved humanity and is largely now unaccountable for its actions. Much of its power comes from the concept of "limited liability" where owners have very little risk but gain high rewards. There also exists the religious-like devotion to quarterly profits, the hoarding of such profits by upper management, the exploitation of workers, and the ability to obtain massive, low interest credit on favorable terms for continued expansion and growth. For human society to continue, and for the planet to flourish, the de-escalation of the power of corporations and the movement away from predatory capitalism must occur. Those seeking Humanity-at-its-Best must work towards this goal. John Maynard Keynes opined about the lack of ethics in capitalism when he said: "Capitalism is the extraordinary belief that the nastiest of men, for the nastiest of motives will somehow work for the benefit of all."

So, what should the future workplace look like if we are to move away from capitalism? No name or "ism" needs to be created. The new workplace needs to remove the hierarchical structure of capitalism and move towards a worker-controlled environment. Power should be decentralized. Instead of striving for never ending short run profits, the drive of businesses should be focused on a healthy planet and a healthy community. Cutthroat competition should be replaced by managed cooperation. It is still permissible for a business to pursue profits to maintain employment for workers and to provide needed products for the community. However, any profits earned should be equally shared amongst all the workers of a business and be reinvested in the community.

Until more just relations are established in the workplace between owners and workers, the "Mandate from Heaven" philosophy should also be applied to the work environment. The current owners of a business should work tirelessly to create a safe and humanizing workplace. Pay and benefits should be sufficient so that workers do not need to go to the state to seek help. Workers are not machines and should be given frequent breaks to eat, hydrate, and use the restroom when needed. Businesses should reinvest in the community through the hiring of needed workers, charitable contributions, and not despoiling the local environment. Owners of businesses should not ask workers to complete tasks or to work in conditions that they themselves would not do- including tasks and work that is degrading or humiliating.

If a business is adhering to the principles of Humanity-at-its-Best the workers then have a duty to support the business by diligently showing up to work on time, completing required tasks, and supporting the business in an ethical way. If the business begins to ignore striving for Humanity-at-its-Best, then the worker has a duty to call out the abuse to other workers and to demand an end to the offense. If the issue is not resolved, the employee has a duty to make the public aware of the grievance, and to seek employment elsewhere. If the owners threaten workers and the community by attempting to relocate the business elsewhere so that they can continue to engage in unethical practices, then the community shall have the right to assume ownership of the business.

It should be understood that leaving dishonorable work and seeking honorable work is not easy, especially for workers living in poorer countries or poorer areas. But progress in reducing the suffering of workers and the destruction of the environment will not occur until enough individuals resist the injustices of the workplace and are joined by other workers in demonstrating solidarity in achieving the goals of Humanity-at-its-Best. Bringing justice to the workplace is a necessary step in addressing and eliminating poverty and inequality. This element of Humanity-at-its-Best is also consistent with the Buddha's requirement in the Eightfold Path of "right livelihood."

Cross-Cultural Quotes in Support of a Harmonious
Relationship With the World of Work

"To be wealthy and honored in an unjust society is a
disgrace." - K'ung Fu-tzu Confucius

"Never get so busy making a living that you forget
to make a life." – Dolly Parton

"Goodness and hard work are rewarded with
respect." – Luther Campbell

"Well done, is better than well said." - Benjamin
Franklin

"From each according to his abilities, to each
according to his needs." - Karl Marx, The Criticism
of the Gotha Program

"Labor is prior to, and independent of, capital.
Capital is only the fruit of labor and could never have
existed if labor had not first existed. Labor is the
superior of capital and deserves much the higher
consideration." Abraham Lincoln - First Annual
Message to Congress, December 3, 1861

"All labor that uplifts humanity has dignity and
importance and should be undertaken with
painstaking excellence." - Martin Luther King Jr.

"The end of labor is to gain leisure"- Aristotle

"Genius begins great works. Labor alone finishes
them." —Joseph Joubert

"Your employees are your brothers upon whom
Allah has given you authority, so if a Muslim has
another person under his control, he/she should feed
them with the like of what one eats and clothe them
with the like of what one wears and you should not
overburden them with what they cannot bear and if
you do so, help them in their jobs."- the Prophet
Muhammad

Work is good, so long as you don't forget to live -
African proverb
You work to live, not live to work. - unknown

"The Sixth Relationship: Achieving a Harmonious Relationship with the Government"

Despite the efforts of individuals to achieve Humanity-at-its-Best, human society will not be able to reach its full potential until harmony exists between the government and the people that have created it. K'ung Fu-tzu (Confucius) warned that governments will fall into chaos and social upheaval if there is no harmony between subject and ruler. Ancient Chinese philosophy relied upon the concept of the Mandate from Heaven- wherein a ruler's authority to govern the people is bestowed from the Heavens. If a ruler fails to govern justly and employs against the people all forms of abuse of power, the mandate to rule is then removed. Most uprisings against a Chinese dynasty were carried out with the belief that the ruler had lost their mandate to govern due to the rise of disorder, usually through some form of corruption.

A more secular version of the Mandate from Heaven was authored by Thomas Jefferson in the Declaration of Independence where he stated that: *"...Governments are instituted among Men, deriving their just powers from the consent of the governed."* Jefferson was influenced by the English philosopher John Locke. Locke put forth the idea that legitimate government only existed by the consent of autonomous individuals who willingly surrendered the right to decide disputes and relinquished that power to rulers who would then make laws for the well-being of the community. The powers of the government became a "contract" granted by the collective will of the people to members of the community to make wise and just decisions on their behalf. The rights of the people did not come from the government, but instead the right to govern came from the people.

All forms of government throughout history have failed at governing justly. They all have disappointed the "Heavens" and those who gave their consent to be ruled. Henry David Thoreau stated in his work Civil Disobedience that: "government is best which governs least"; and… "That government is best which governs not at all"; and when men are prepared for it, that will be the kind of government which they will have." Many who have read this phrase have focused on the beginning part (governing least) to advocate for limited government. But limited government won't happen unless we focus on the latter part (...and when men are prepared for it). This is why it is important for practitioners of Humanity-at-its-Best to get their own house in order, before they can make claims to be a candidate for political office. If greedy and corrupt people occupy office, then there will be disharmony. Harmony can only be obtained if office holders are those seeking Humanity-at-its-Best. To paraphrase Gandhi: "It is better to be a politician trying to be a saint, instead of a saint trying to be a politician." It would be best for society if a move could be made from representative democracy to direct democracy.

Although it is preferable for those seeking Humanity-at-its-Best to influence government from the outside by demanding politicians serve the people through pursuing justice and harmony, they may choose to offer themselves as a public office holder. If a practitioner of Humanity-at-its-Best decides to occupy public office the following guidelines need to be observed:

No membership in an organized political party. Candidates need to remain independent. This requirement is necessary to ensure office holders serve the needs of the people instead of the needs of a political party.

Salary capped at the medium income level of the district (local, state, federal) being represented. Salaries can be raised only when the income for the citizens being represented increases. Any difference in pay should be donated to food banks or homeless shelters.

    a. It would be best to have campaigns publicly financed. Until that time, donations are to be limited to the daily income of a minimum wage worker in the district. Donations may only be accepted from individuals. No donations may be accepted from corporations, organizations, PACs, etc… This is to ensure that the interests of the people are served.

    b. Office holders may not serve more than two consecutive terms. This is mainly to ward off bribes and complacency. It also protects against a practitioner from developing an inflated ego thinking they are the only one that can do a good job in holding the office.

A study of history has shown that all governments throughout history, whatever their form, have been controlled by a small ruling elite who use the reins of government to increase their wealth and power and to impoverish and subjugate the majority. To maintain its privileged position, the ruling elite uses all governing tools available to suppress the citizenry. Therefore, it can be accurately stated that all governments have fought and continue to fight a war against a common enemy: their own citizens. The ruling elites recently have been largely successful in preventing the masses from realizing the war being waged against them because of the use of highly effective propaganda. This means those seeking Humanity-at-its-Best must always take the side of the citizens who seek justice in their lives over the ruling elite who seek injustice.

So how should the private citizen seeking Humanity-at-its-Best relate to the government which rules over them? There is no obligation to obey the government if the government acts unjustly. When the state acts to serve the interests of the ruling elite over the interests of the people, it has lost its mandate to rule. There is no obligation for citizens to sacrifice their time, livelihoods, or personal safety for a government that is plagued by unjust rule and corruption. Those seeking Humanity-at-its-Best should resist corrupt governments by engaging in civil disobedience. Any government that refuses to pursue justice and equality has forfeited its power to rule and is therefore illegitimate. When a government has lost its legitimacy, citizens are no longer obligated to respect and obey such a government. Those seeking Humanity-at-its-Best must always call out injustice policies and corrupt practices in all governments because honor and integrity demand it.

It is easy to call out for improvements in foreign countries. But it is especially important to highlight the faults of one's home country, for that is where the ability to affect change is strongest. Great courage will be needed since demanding the end of unjust policies will produce resentment from fellow citizens. As Plato said, "no one is more hated than he who speaks the truth."

In modern times governments have used patriotism to cloak their illegal and corrupt activities. For the person seeking Humanity-at-its Best, it is acceptable to be patriotic if the definition is limited to being proud of past noble acts and showing love towards the city, state, or country of residence. It is not acceptable to be nationalistic. There is no room for supporting harmful nationalistic policies and destructive wars. Those in pursuit of Humanity-at-its-Best understand that people in every country in the world are interested in being gainfully employed, while trying to make enough money to raise a family and to find some joy in their lives. Most wars throughout history-and all modern wars- have been fought to increase the wealth, power and status of the ruling elites and their supporters. Governments and the corporations which control them are the ones who desire war. People everywhere want peace. All governments should be pushed by their peoples to pursue peace through all available channels, including international ones such as the United Nations Charter. If government representatives are following the guidelines of Humanity-at-its-Best, then war should not occur, as the principles of empathy, non-violence, honor, civility, and integrity would not allow it.

There can be no support for modern wars which are

fought for the interests of wealthy individuals, profits for powerful corporations, or forced conversions by adherents of unholy religions. Those practicing Humanity-at-its-Best should resist the appeals of war mongers and seek their removal from office.

Just as it is vital that those pursuing Humanity-at-its-Best conduct self-examinations to discover individual weaknesses, faulty beliefs, or areas of improvement, so too, should examinations be made of the city, state, or country one resides in. The duty of every resident is to be vigilant in demanding justice and accountability for all government officials. This is why it is accurate to say that citizens who criticize those in power are the most patriotic. American author and critic James Baldwin articulated this when he stated: "I love America more than any other country in the world and, exactly for this reason, I insist on the right to criticize her perpetually." Conversely, those who refuse to criticize the injustice of their governments and their officials are the least patriotic. For those seeking Humanity-at-its-Best, it thus becomes necessary to become a dissident. Dissidents differ from nationalists in that they focus their criticism on the governments in which they are residents and citizens of. That is where they can affect the most change. Being a dissident is in alignment with Jesus's warning that we should not be "concerned about the speck in our neighbor's eye but be more concerned about the log in our own."

Every city, state, or country has a sinful and corrupt past. The sins and corruption of the past have shaped the present and will influence the future unless there is an awareness, accountability, and reconciliation process which addresses these crimes.

Those in power will resist such a process as they benefit from the corruption of nationalistic and greed-based policies. They will attempt to suppress any teaching of a nation's history which tries to shed light on the crimes committed in the name of nationalism and patriotism. There is a correlation between nationalism and historical illiteracy. Since all nations have a sinful past, it is accurate to say that the more nationalistic a person is, the more illiterate that person is of their country's history. Therefore, adherents to Humanity-at-its-Best must reject all appeals to nationalism as they are being made by people who are uninformed. There will not be peace on this planet until nationalism is eradicated and universal brotherhood recognized.

A careful examination of the role of government in human affairs is that it has been used as a tool of the ruling elites to suppress the will of the majority. It is essential that the seeker of Humanity-at-its-Best recognize the power dynamic that shapes human society. The imbalance of power is an old story. The Greek philosopher Thucydides warned, "The strong do what they can and the weak suffer what they must." The goal then is to create a government where power is decentralized. All forms of government have been ruled by corrupt, ruling elites. This reality means that every person striving for Humanity-at-its-Best must be active in fighting to end injustice against the masses who are being exploited. A government following the principles of Humanity-at-its-Best will notice a decline in poverty, inequality, corruption and injustice.

Cross-Cultural Quotes in Support of a Harmonious Relationship with the Government

"In a country well governed, poverty is something to be ashamed of. In a country badly governed, wealth is something to be ashamed of."- K'ung Fu-tzu (Confucius)

"Justice is a moral physician and cures men of their excesses and makes them better people." - Socrates in Plato's *Gorgias*

"History will judge societies and governments — and their institutions — not by how big they are or how well they serve the rich and the powerful, but by how effectively they respond to the needs of the poor and the helpless." - Cesar Chavez

"Corruption is the enemy of development, and of good governance. It must be got rid of. Both the government and the people at large must come together to achieve this national objective. - Prativha Pathil

"Government is a trust, and the officers of the government are trustees. And both the trust and the trustees are created for the benefit of the people." - Henry Clay

"Government of the people, by the people, for the people, shall not perish from the Earth." - Abraham Lincoln

"When the ruler of a country is just and good, the ministers become just and good; when the ministers are just and good, the higher officials become just and good; when the higher officials are just and good, the rank and file become just and good; when the rank and file become just and good, the people become just and good." - Buddha

"Being just for one hour in government is better than worshiping for sixty years." - the Prophet Muhammad

"When it can be said by any country in the world, my poor are happy, neither ignorance nor distress is to be found among them, my jails are empty of prisoners, my streets of beggars, the aged are not in want, the taxes are not oppressive, the rational world is my friend because I am the friend of happiness. When these things can be said, then may that country boast its constitution and government."- Thomas Paine

"In Iroquois society, leaders are encouraged to remember seven generations in the past and consider seven generations in the future when making decisions that affect the people."- Wilma Mankiller

"The Seventh Relationship: Achieving a Harmonious Relationship with the Unknown"

Humans have always been in awe of the mysteries of the world and their place in the universe. The "unknown" is a term used to describe the centuries old inquiry into the questions of how an individual comes into existence in the universe and what happens to a person when they die. Throughout history organized religion has provided answers to these questions. But for those seeking Humanity-at-its-Best, the "certainty" and "conviction of faith" of organized religion becomes an obstacle in the pursuit of the "unknown."

The Buddha asked his followers to be a "lamp upon yourself." He is asking people to have the courage to forge their own path to discovering the truth. It requires individuals to use a system of questioning and testing to discover authentic and wise teachings. This makes organized religion, with its demand of obediently accepting established dogma, unsuitable for those seeking enlightenment or for those striving for Humanity-at-its-Best.

So how does a person seeking Humanity-at-its-Best accommodate the ever-present influence of organized religion? For those seeking to improve themselves, it is a matter of separating the "wheat from the chaff." This means those seeking Humanity-at-its-Best may incorporate the philosophical and ethical principles from organized religion which are in alignment with the principles of seeking Humanity-at-its-Best, while ignoring and discarding those beliefs and practices which promote discrimination, violence and submission to the power structure of a religion.

Jesus warned his disciples about the futility in trying to "serve two masters." That advice serves those seeking Humanity-at-its-Best. A person cannot serve the interests of an organized religion and at the same time be an independent seeker of truth. If someone is pursuing Humanity-at-its-Best and is publicly also known to serve an organized religion, and if a conflict in doctrine or a social crisis arises, there may be demands put on the seeker of Humanity-at-its-Best to abandon its principles and side with the organized religion. Such a decision might temporarily benefit the organized religion, but it would have negative, long-term consequences with the general public losing confidence in the principles of Humanity-at-its-Best. Therefore, individuals seeking Humanity-at-its-Best should avoid subscribing to and becoming an adherent of an organized religion. Adherents should seek to be spiritual (an individual search for harmony and peace) instead of religious (subscribing to an enforced, collective belief system or dogma).

Those seeking Humanity-at-its-Best should also abstain from joining or publicly endorsing theistic religions. Theism, which promotes the idea of a god that plays an active role in human affairs, prevents those seeking Humanity-at-its-Best from discovering the truth for two reasons. The first reason is that theistic religions demand that their adherents strictly follow the dogma of the faith and the pronouncements of the religion's hierarchy. Failure to do so gets one labeled a heretic. It also does not allow for individual discernment of the truth, which is the foundation for those seeking Humanity-at-its-Best. There can be no division of loyalties between serving a religion and pursuing Humanity-at-its-Best. Therefore, the person seeking Humanity-at-its-Best must not lose independence of belief and action which means there can be no membership and adherence to organized religion.

The second reason to avoid theism is that it has as a foundational belief that God takes an active role in human affairs and that God makes his/her/its desires and plans knowable to humanity. The belief that man can understand god's thoughts has been one of the main problems that has plagued humanity giving religious leaders and rulers the excuse and ability to cause enormous suffering through the ages. Since no human mind could comprehend the thoughts of an omnipotent being, all the death and suffering imposed on humanity has been the responsibility of the charlatans and grifters who have used the belief of a direct connection between man and God for personal gain. For humanity to advance, theism needs to perish. Those pursuing Humanity-at-its-Best must not subscribe to theism, but instead work towards its ending. The words of Voltaire are important here: "Those who can make you believe absurdities; can make you commit atrocities." Humanity needs to evolve to the point where when some person claims: "God told me…" or "God commands us to…" or "it is God's will…" that everyone present will say "Stop! Neither you nor anyone else can ever know the thoughts of an omnipotent God. The thoughts of a "supreme being" which controls the movements of every celestial body in the universe, unrestricted by time and place, possessing the power to create and destroy, is beyond human comprehension. Therefore, what you claim cannot possibly be true. Clinging to a belief that you can communicate with an omnipotent being is a clear sign of either suffering from a mental illness or being a sociopath." Those pursuing Humanity-at-its-Best, therefore, may not identify with theism, but may identify with deism, agnosticism, or atheism.

A final aspect of the unknown that deserves attention is the pursuit to expand our knowledge and presence in the faraway systems and galaxies of space. Achieving such a goal cannot be entertained until the human species has achieved universal adherence to the principles of Humanity-at-its-Best. If we are to make contact with intelligent and compassionate life forms, then the human race needs to clean up its act first. Currently, we have very little to offer as evidence that we are worthy of belonging to an association of planets that engages in the promotion of life and the expansion of knowledge. Any alien species arriving at our planet would feel disgust at the condition of our biosphere. All humanity should feel deep shame at how we have despoiled a paradise. Other planets and civilizations would be justified in quarantining our species to not leave our solar system until we have embraced non-violence, compassion, and empathy as the guiding principles in human affairs while also restoring the planet's health.

Cross-Cultural Quotes in Support of a Harmonious Relationship with the Unknown

Just as a candle cannot burn without fire, men cannot live without a spiritual life. - Buddha

Peace comes within the souls of men, when they realize their oneness with the Universe, when they realize it is really everywhere... it is within each one of us. - Black Elk

"Character can not be developed in ease and quiet. Only through experience of trial and suffering can the soul be strengthened, ambition inspired, and success achieved." – Helen Keller

"Spiritual growth is not like fast food. It takes time for its roots to grow, and that requires us to be receptive and patient." – Rabbi Zalman Schachter-Shalom

"Make your own Bible. Select and collect all the words and sentences that in all your readings have been to you like the blast of a trumpet." – Ralph Waldo Emerson

"Whatever is true, whatever is noble, whatever is right, whatever is pure, whatever is lovely, whatever is admirable—if anything is excellent or praiseworthy—think about such things." – Philippians 4:8

"Knowledge is like a garden. If it is not cultivated, it cannot be harvested." - African Proverb

"There is only one corner of the universe you can be certain of improving, and that's your own self." - Aldous Huxley

"Our planet is a lonely speck in the great enveloping cosmic dark. In our obscurity, in all this vastness, there is no hint that help will come from elsewhere to save us from ourselves."- Carl Sagan

"By three methods we may learn wisdom: First, by reflection, which is noblest; Second, by imitation, which is easiest; and third by experience, which is the bitterest." - K'ung Fu-tzu (Confucius)

"Keep me away from the wisdom which does not cry, the philosophy which does not laugh and the greatness which does not bow before children." - Kahlil Gibran

Chapter Three
How the Tools and Relationships for Humanity-at-its-Best Can Be Used to Achieve a Noble Life

For someone striving to attain Humanity-at-its-Best the tools and relationships outlined above provide a **general** roadmap to living harmoniously with others (humans, animals, the earth). But what about the **"specifics"** in life? This next section will be devoted to providing guidance in areas of everyday life. In some respects, this section will be like the "suras" of Islam, which guide the adherent to understanding the subject matter of the Koran.

Money, Property, and Wealth

A useful starting point might be Aristotle's description of the difference between "natural" wealth and "artificial" wealth. Aristotle posits that the owning of property/money/wealth that is used to provide a family a means of existing "comfortably" (meeting required human needs) is acceptable. Natural wealth also benefits the state indirectly through a stable and secure citizenry. Artificial wealth on the other hand, is the use of money to accumulate more wealth for purposes beyond the needs of maintaining a comfortable household. Examples of artificial wealth are usury, speculation, and rent seeking activities that profit on the misfortunes of fellow members of the community. Artificial wealth does not benefit the state but rather the interests of the wealthy few who tend to use their wealth to dominate their neighbors. We can therefore classify artificial wealth as "unnatural" and base in its motivations, while natural wealth is noble and in concert with striving for Humanity-at-its-Best.

The acquisition of natural wealth is in harmony with many of the relationships discussed previously. By living moderately in one's household, the seeker of Humanity-at-its-Best secures a strong bond with humanity at large (relationship 1) through the emphasis on empathy, as well as members of the local community (relationship 2) through the emphasis on moderation.

For those seeking Humanity-at-its-Best working in both the private and the public sector, the same guidelines to pay and benefits outlined above for those seeking public office should be followed (Salary capped at the medium income level of the district (local, state, federal) being adhered to. Salaries can be raised only when the income for the citizens being represented increases. Any difference in pay should be donated to food banks or homeless shelters.) For those in professions that require extensive educational degrees that are expensive to obtain, a debt repayment/cancellation plan should be worked out with the employer or the government. The same principle should apply to the acquisition of property. For example, the residential accommodations one lives in should not exceed the medium price for homes/apartments, etc... Those seeking Humanity-at-its-Best should avoid investing their financial resources in ventures that are deemed harmful to the environment or to the larger human community.

The Buddha provides important guidance when it comes to the accumulation of wealth. "We do not possess our home, our children, or even our own body. They are only given to us for a short while to treat with care and respect."

Reputation and Recognition

Those seeking Humanity-at-its-Best should avoid seeking recognition for their choices and their actions. Service to the global/local community and to the environment is the inner reward that provides meaning and comfort. No titles should be used or sought out. Such titles serve to provide a social ranking in a hierarchical society. It is better to use titles that denote equality, such as "citizen", "comrade", "brother" or "seeker."

What is important in holding a position or employment in an occupation is the honorable discharge of one's duties and the maintenance of personal integrity. If this is successfully accomplished, one will gain self-respect as a personal reward.

When practicing Humanity-at-its-Best the adherent should strive to not bring shame to others who are also striving for the same goal. If one cannot publicly live up to the principles of Humanity-at-its-Best, then one should disassociate oneself from fellow practitioners and to focus on self-improvement privately. The ability to rejoin after meditation and practice is always available.

In terms of notoriety and fame, those seeking Humanity-at-its-Best should follow the advice of the sage K'ung Fu-tzu (Confucius) where he states, "Do not worry that you are unknown, but rather seek to be worth knowing." An adherent's actions will define their reputation. If a person striving for Humanity-at-its-Best achieves a measure of fame and popularity, it is imperative that the person not attempt to "cash in" and make money on their notoriety. There is no honor in getting paid to advertise and promote a product or service. If a person believes that something is useful to the community, they will humbly explain why and not receive payment of any kind.

And how should an adherent to Humanity-at-its-Best be recognized by the public? The public will know the practitioner by inspired actions and words, by devotion to the elimination of injustice, by humbly serving the less fortunate in the community, and by the avoidance of accumulating wealth and property. But it may be helpful to the community to wear some easily recognizable marker or symbol to signify one's status as a seeker of Humanity-at-its-Best. The symbol can be displayed on an article of clothing, a bracelet, chain or other accessory as deemed fit. This symbol should be displayed when engaging with the public. It is predictable that some "wolves in sheep's clothing" will attempt to disparage those seeking to live by the principles of Humanity-at-its-Best. Every organization has had to deal with such imposters. That is why the actions of a person striving for Humanity-at-its-Best are of such paramount importance.

The public will also be able to recognize a person striving for Humanity-at-its-best because the

adherents:
- Are humble and not arrogant
-Engage in moral self-reflection
-Seek out dialogue with community members to increase wisdom
- Seek to increase the standard of living of the masses of workers, and not the ruling elites
- acknowledge past injustices while also working to eliminate present injustices
- support the application of non-violence, empathy, and reason as a first resort to solving social issues
- seeks cooperative methods of solving social issues over competitive ones
- engages in actions that are noble and honorable, while rejecting those that are base and dishonorable

Chapter Four
What Does Practicing Humanity-at-its-Best Help You to Attain?

There are both personal and societal benefits for those who seek Humanity-at-its-Best. Seekers utilizing the tools described above should notice over time an increase in knowledge and wisdom. The desire for enlightenment and wisdom is driven by the recognition that society is plagued by violence and corruption and that the ills of society cannot be confronted until individuals do the hard work of presenting themselves as trustworthy and honorable candidates to assist the masses in transformative change. Such an undertaking will bring rewards, but those rewards will not be realized until the adherent begins the arduous work of stripping away the biases, prejudices, myths, and propaganda that society has created around them. This task can best be accomplished by persistent dialogue, moral reflection, and meditation.

Adherents should be aware that when they first set out on the path of Humanity-at-its-Best they will encounter resistance from those closest to them. This is natural for anyone striving for self-improvement. Patience, understanding, and humility are what is needed to weather the storm. Those individuals in our historical past who have attempted to improve themselves have all sought to expand their knowledge. The knowledge they acquired was combined with experience to produce wisdom. The pursuit of wisdom is a common trait found in all historical figures who have striven to improve their societies. These individuals used their acquired wisdom to demand a more just society. This is also the main driving force behind those seeking Humanity-at-its-Best.

The pursuit of wisdom requires humility in the face of ignorance. Socrates stated that the only thing he knew for sure was that he knew nothing. The path to wisdom necessitates that each individual should question the narrative created by the society one lives in and to conduct a daily self- examination of one's beliefs. Socrates insisted that an unexamined life is not worth living. Mencius, a Confucian philosopher, realized that too few members of society engage in self-reflection when he stated, "To act without understanding and to do so habitually without examination, following certain courses all their lives without seeing the underlying reasons -- such is the way of the masses."

When engaging in dialogue with another person it is important to remember to not fall for traps such as engaging in debate with someone who does not provide evidence to back up their claims. Evidence free statements and debates are meant to obfuscate and sidetrack honest inquiry. What is asserted without evidence may be dismissed without evidence.

The path to achieving Humanity-at-its-Best is a journey that spans the life course of a person. It should begin with the instruction of children. This should begin at home with parents serving as examples as well as providing the initial instruction to the principles of Humanity-at-its-Best. This instruction should continue in whatever school setting a child enters. As a person enters adulthood, the search for knowledge and serving one's community should be pursued over the search for profit. Travel should be encouraged so that the interconnectivity of all life can be witnessed. Occupations should be sought out that are honorable and benefit the community over those occupations where profit and higher wages are deemed more important than service to the community. If those seeking Humanity- at- its-Best wish to begin a family, then both the parents and the community need to provide more time and resources for the healthy development of the child. As the adherent to Humanity-at-its-Best enters their golden years, there should be a transition from a wage paying occupation to community supportive activities such as taking care of elderly parents, helping to raise grandchildren, teaching the principles of Humanity-at-its-Best, and tending to Mother Earth. Let us follow the advice of an ancient Greek proverb that says: "A society grows great when old men plant trees whose shade they know they shall never sit in."

What should be the end result of individuals and nations practicing Humanity-at-its-Best? There are many historical sources of wisdom to draw upon to answer this question but perhaps a quote from Crazy Horse best surmises the goal: "I see a time of Seven Generations when all the colors of mankind will gather under the Sacred Tree of Life and the whole Earth will become one circle again." We must always strive to live in harmony with the planet we reside on. If each person in a family practices Humanity-at-its-Best then the family is improved. If each family in a community practices Humanity-at-its-Best then the community is improved. If each community practices Humanity-at-its-Best, then the nation is improved. If each nation practices Humanity-at-its-Best, then the entire world is improved. If the whole world is practicing Humanity-at-its-Best, then justice and harmony are achieved.

Afterword

After reading through the pages above, the seeker of Humanity-at-its-Best might agree with the principles but decide that the work to achieve them is too difficult. That only mystics, monks, and scholarly academics could have the fortitude to persevere with such an endeavor. But such thinking would only be true if one is only focused on the final destination, instead of the journey. It is true that the search for justice requires a stoic steadfastness. But there is also room for experiencing the wonders that life provides.

Truth and justice are the roots and trunk of the human tree. The fruits of such a tree are joy, equanimity, solidarity, and humor. These soul nourishing fruits are the result of the labor in the pursuit and cultivation of truth and justice. The countless multitudes who have strived for justice over the centuries have known this because, in their absence, it becomes difficult to taste these life sustaining fruits. One does not need to be cloistered away in serious study inside a cell in a monastery or constantly engaged in civic protest to experience the benefits of pursuing justice. It can also be felt in helping a member of the community, celebrating with friends at a local festival, or rejuvenating oneself in the bosom of nature.

Let us begin our journey together by following the

inspirational advice from a poem by Henry Wadsworth Longfellow:

Let us, then, be up and doing,
With a heart for any fate;
Still achieving, still pursuing,
Learn to labor and to wait.

About the Author

Glenn Hoffarth is the son of working-class parents who attended a small, public university in Wisconsin. He later earned a master's degree in history and then taught for over thirty years at a state technical college. He is currently retired.